CAMBRIDGE
SHIRE
COUNTRY RECIPES

COMPILED BY
PIPPA GOMAR

ℛℛ
RAVETTE BOOKS

Published by Ravette Limited,
3 Glenside Estate, Star Road,
Partridge Green, Horsham,
Sussex RH13 8RA
(0403) 710392

Production: Oval Projects Ltd.
Cover Design: Jim Wire
Printing & binding: Nørhaven AS

All recipes are given in Imperial and Metric
weights and measures. Where measurements
are given in 'cups', these are American cups,
holding 8 fluid ounces.

The recipes contained in this book are traditional
and many have been compiled from archival sources.
Every effort has been made to ensure that the recipes
are correct.

RECIPES

MEAT

PUDDINGS

CAKES AND BREAD

PRESERVES

SAUCES

STUFFINGS

DRINKS

CAMBRIDGESHIRE

Cambridgeshire is a predominantly flat county, with fertile farmland on which crops and stock flourish.

Reclaimed from the sea, the fenland area of the county is rich in peat and humus from prehistoric forests, and its huge, hedgeless fields produce cabbage, celery and root crops in abundance. On the islands formed by the high ground before the sea was pushed back, villages became established which can be identified by names ending with the suffix 'ea' or 'ey' ('y'). Ely, still known as 'the Isle of Ely', was once such an island. Famous for its cathedral, it is the centre of one of the richest agricultural areas in Britain. For the people living in the isolated fenland communities, survival became a matter of fishing and hunting to supplement their meagre diet. Eels were plentiful, and became popular in cooking, as, too, did rabbits, hares and wildfowl. Birds such as sparrows, larks and blackbirds were commonly snared and eaten in pies and puddings.

In the south of the county, and around Cambridge itself, the soil is ideal for fruit, and strawberries, gooseberries, pears and apples grow in abundance. Just outside Cambridge is the village of Over, which was the centre of butter-making. Until as recently as the early 1900s, butter was sold in the city from wicker baskets in rolls a yard (90cm) long, an inch (2.5cm) thick and weighing 1 lb (450g).

The west of the county, around Huntingdon, is still a rich agricultural area where crops such as wheat, barley and oats particularly flourish. Not unnaturally, bread formed a major part of the diet of the country people. It was traditionally baked on Fridays, in long wooden troughs, and in the poorest households it formed the basis of 'delights' such as milk sop or water mess. Milk sop was a slice of bread, seasoned with salt and pepper, over which milk was poured. Water mess was similar, but with water replacing the milk. These dishes were usually served for breakfast or supper.

A thick slice of bread, perhaps thinly spread with butter or cheese, was lunch for the farm labourer. Known as a 'docky' - because the time taken to eat it was docked from a man's wages - it was cut into mouthfuls with a 'docky knife'. During harvest time, the 'docky' would be supplemented during the afternoon by 'cakes and ale'.

Cambridgeshire is well known for its ales, which are brewed from local barley. Farmers and ordinary house-holders, too, brewed their own beer for domestic consumption; homemade wine was also popular, for serving at christenings, weddings and funerals.

Blue-veined Stilton cheese, although now usually associated with Melton Mowbray, in Leicestershire, actually takes its name from the village of Stilton, which is situated on the Great North Road. It was first popularised in the 18th century by the Bell Inn at Stilton, where it was enjoyed by the many travellers who passed through the village. But traditional Cambridgeshire cheese is soft and brick-shaped, with its sides higher than the centre. It is unseasoned, and, when served, is broken up with a fork and then seasoned with salt, pepper and vinegar.

Cambridgeshire was once a county of sharply contrasting eating habits. To the north, the isolation of the fenland people forced them to rely on local produce, from which they created simple dishes.

The relatively heavily-populated city of Cambridge and its University, on the other hand, attracted a variety of produce from a wide surrounding area, so it was a place in which more elaborate dishes could be enjoyed. The culinary delights of the University, such as Welsh Venison, tended to be rich as well as varied. Many of these dishes, once traditional to the colleges, have become very popular as generations of undergraduates have spread their renown throughout the country. Nowadays the old contrast in eating habits has almost disappeared as better distribution had made modern foods easily accessible to everybody.

But the county can offer other fascinating contrasts, from the elegance of Cambridge to the bleakness of places such as Wicken Fen where the visitor can still gain a clear idea of what it was like to live in the fens before the land was reclaimed.

A warm June evenin': a-gard'nin'; a lark in the sky;
Earth on m'hands; a kitten a-playin' nearby;
Mart'ns a-burblin', clingin' there high on the wall;
Sweet peas, an' pansies, an' carrots, an' celery, an' all ...
Scent o' the pinks, an' the roses; an' yew settin' there
Runnin' orf honey, like amber ...

John Kett

SPRING SOUP

This recipe from Cambridge dates back to the early 19th Century.

3 large onions
1 oz (25 g) butter
1 lettuce
1 lb (450 g) fresh or frozen peas
$^1/_2$ pint (300 ml/ 1$^1/_4$ cups) water
1 tablespoon each of parsley, sorrel, chervil,
    purslane (freshly chopped)
Salt and pepper
$^1/_2$ pint (300 ml/ 1$^1/_4$ cups) milk
A little extra parsley or
    a few purslane flowers to decorate

Chop the onions and put them in a large saucepan with the butter.

Cook them until they are soft and golden.

Shred the lettuce and add this to the onions.

Add the peas and just enough water to cover the vegetables.

Add the herbs and season with salt and pepper.

Cook gently until the peas are tender.

Strain off the liquid and keep on one side.

Purée or sieve the vegetables and put them back in the pan with the liquid.

Mix the egg yolks and the milk in another saucepan and heat until it thickens.

Gradually add the milk mixture to the vegetable mixture, stirring all the time.

Heat gently but do not boil.

Serve decorated with a little parsley or purslane flowers.

MARROW SOUP

During the Middle Ages soups made with vegetables and served with bread formed a substantial part of the diet of country folk during the winter months.

1 lb (450 g) vegetable marrow
2 oz (50 g) butter
1 onion
1 stick of celery
2 carrots
1 small turnip
1 oz (25 g) flour
2 pints (1.15 litres/ 5 cups) white stock
Salt and pepper
$^{1}/_{4}$ pint (150 ml/ $^{2}/_{3}$ cup) double cream

Peel the marrow, cut it in half and scoop out the seeds.

Dice the marrow flesh.

Chop the onion, celery, carrots and turnip.

Gently cook them in the butter in a covered saucepan for 10 minutes, without letting them go brown.

Add the flour and cook for a few more minutes.

Gradually add the stock, stirring all the time.

Simmer gently for 30-40 minutes or until the vegetables are really tender.

Blend in a liquidizer or rub through a wire sieve.

Season with salt and pepper.

Stir in the cream and re-heat the soup but do not let it boil.

EEL BROTH

Eels were plentiful on the fens at the time of the construction of
Ely Cathedral. They were used to make soups and pottages up until
the end of the 19th century. This is a late Victorian recipe.

1 lb (450 g) eels
1¹/₂ pints (900 ml/ 3³/₄ cups) water
2 blades of mace
A strip of lemon peel
A few peppercorns
Salt
Bouquet garni
2 onions
2 oz (50 g) butter
2 oz (50 g) flour
¹/₂ pint (300 ml/ 1¹/₄ cups) milk
2 egg yolks

Put the water, mace, lemon peel, peppercorns, salt, eels and
bouquet garni into a large saucepan.

Boil until the eel meat is tender (when the flesh just comes
away from the bone).

Remove the eels, take out the bones and remove the heads.

Reserve the eel stock.

Chop the onions and fry them in the butter.

Add the flour to make a roux and cook for a few minutes.

Gradually add the eel stock.

Remove the bouquet garni and lemon peel. Add the milk.

Chop the eel meat into small cubes and add to the stock.

Mix the egg yolks with two tablespoons of cooled stock,
then add to the broth. Heat and serve.

PORT AND STILTON MOUSSE

4 oz (100 g) Stilton cheese without the rind
¼ pint (150 ml/ ⅔ cup) milk
¼ pint (150 ml/ ⅔ cup) port
½ oz (15 g) gelatine
½ pint (300 ml/ 1¼ cups) double cream
2 egg whites
Salt and pepper

Blend the Stilton and the milk in a liquidizer.

Mix the gelatine with the port, leave for a few minutes and then heat slowly until the gelatine dissolves.

Mix the gelatine and the port into the Stilton and milk.

Season with salt and pepper.

Whisk the cream until thick and fold in.

Whisk the egg whites until stiff and fold in.

Pour into ramekins or bowls and chill in the fridge.

Serve with melba toast or granary bread.

MOUSSE OF SALMON

Serves 4-6

This mousse was served at the oldest University college in Cambridge, Peterhouse, in the 1920s. Then it was served on a platter surrounded by gull's eggs, with three gull's eggs for each serving. As gull's eggs are now rather hard to come by, use hard-boiled chicken's eggs instead.

12 oz (350 g) cooked salmon, skinned, boned and flaked
1/2 pint (300 ml/ 1 1/4 cups) double cream
Juice of half a lemon
Salt and pepper
A pinch of chopped tarragon, fresh or dried
A pinch of nutmeg
3 egg whites
1/4 pint (150 ml/ 2/3 cup) mayonnaise
4-6 hard-boiled eggs
Watercress to decorate

Mash the salmon.

Stir in the cream, lemon juice, salt, pepper, tarragon and nutmeg.

Whisk the egg whites until stiff and fold into the mixture.

Butter a mould and spoon the mixture in, but not right up to the top.

Cover with foil.

Stand in a tin of hot water.

Bake in a moderate oven for 30 minutes.

Turn the mousse out while it is still warm.

Chill in the fridge.

Decorate with the watercress, mayonnaise and hard-boiled eggs.

Oven: 350°F/180°C Gas Mark 4

HUNTINGDON STUFFED PEARS Serves 4

This is a savoury dish that can be served as a starter to a meal.

2 large ripe pears
4 oz (100 g) Stilton cheese
1 oz (25 g) butter
1 tablespoon double cream
Freshly ground black pepper to taste
2 oz (50 g) walnut halves
Juice of half a lemon
A few lettuce leaves

Blend the cheese, butter, cream and pepper together.

Chop most of the walnuts, leaving 4 unchopped for decoration.

Add the walnuts to the cheese mixture.

Peel the pears and cut each in half.

Scoop out the centre of each half.

Brush lemon juice on the pears to prevent discolouration.

Divide the cheese mixture equally between the 4 pear halves

Serve each pear half on a bed of lettuce decorated with the walnuts.

PERCH IN WHITE WINE

Perch were once frequently caught in the fens. Oliver Cromwell's wife, Elizabeth Bourchier, made a similar dish using perch.

4 medium perch
1 wineglassful of white wine
At least 2 pints (1.15 litres/ 5 cups) stock
1 bay leaf
1 onion, sliced
Bouquet garni
1 clove of garlic
Salt and pepper
2 oz (50 g) butter
2 oz (50 g) flour
Fresh parsley

Wash, scale and clean the perch.

Remove the gills.

Put in a large shallow pan and add the wine and stock to cover the fish.

Add the onion, bay leaf, bouquet garni, garlic, salt and pepper.

Simmer gently until the fish is tender.

Remove the fish and keep warm in a dish covered with buttered paper.

Strain the stock.

In another pan melt the butter and add the flour. Cook for a few minutes.

Gradually add the stock and stir over a medium heat until it thickens.

Chop the parsley and add it to the sauce.

Serve the fish covered with the sauce.

GRILLED HERRINGS

Serves 4

Herrings were traditionally sold at the Stourbridge Fair held annually in Cambridge.

4 fresh herrings 8-12 oz (225 g-350 g) each
Salt and pepper
Oil or bacon fat
A few drops of vinegar

Heat the grill to a moderate heat.

Cut the heads off the herrings.

Split each herring down the back and remove the back bone and as many of the finer bones as possible.

Rub salt inside the fish.

Remove the scales by scraping a knife from the tail to the head.

Make 3 oblique slits in the skin on each side of the fish.

Sprinkle with salt and pepper.

Brush the fish with oil or bacon fat.

Put a few drops of vinegar into each slit.

Put the fish under the grill and cook for about 10 minutes.

Turn the fish over and grill for a further 10 minutes.

Serve immediately with brown bread and butter.

EEL PIE

Eels were once so plentiful that they became a currency. Land rent could be paid to the church or state in 'booklets' or 'sticks' of eels. The monks at Ely exchanged 4,000 eels a year for stone to build Ely Cathedral.

2 lbs (about 1 kg) eel steaks
2 oz (50 g) flour
Salt and pepper
2 oz (50 g) butter
1 onion
1 tablespoon chopped herbs (parsley, tarragon)
Grated rind and juice of 1 lemon
A wineglassful of white wine
1/4 pint (150 ml/ 2/3 cup) cream
8 oz (225 g) puff pastry
A little milk to glaze

Cut the eel steaks into chunks.

Season the flour with salt and pepper. Roll the eel in the flour.

Melt the butter in a frying pan and fry the eel until brown all over. Put the eel in a pie dish.

Chop the onion and fry in the butter. Add the remaining flour and mix with the butter and onion to make a roux.

Add the herbs, lemon rind and juice, and the wine. Cook until it thickens then stir in the cream. Pour the sauce over the eel.

Roll out the pastry and cover the pie dish with it.

Brush the pastry with milk.Bake at the higher temperature for 20 minutes then at the lower temperature for a further 30 to 40 minutes.

Oven: 425°F/220°C Gas Mark 7
Reduce to: 350°F/180°C Gas Mark 4

MRS. BEETON'S STEWED EELS Serves 4

The common eel is a fresh water fish. It can be fried, grilled or poached and is particularly good in soups and stews.

2-2¹/₄ lbs (approximately 1 kg) eels or 4 eel steaks weighing
    about ¹/₂ lb (225 g) each
Salt and pepper
2 onions
4 cloves
A strip of lemon peel
1 pint (600 ml/ 2¹/₂ cups) chicken stock
3 fl oz (75 ml) port
3 fl oz (75 ml) double cream
2 oz (50 g) flour
A pinch of cayenne pepper
A few drops of lemon juice

Whole eels should be washed, skinned and their heads should be removed. Cut them into pieces about 3 inches (7.5 cm) long.

Put the slices of eel or the eel steaks into a large saucepan which will just hold them in one layer.

Season with salt and pepper.

Peel the onions and stick the cloves into them.

Place the onions on the fish.

Add the strip of lemon peel.

Mix the stock and the port in a small saucepan and pour over the fish.

Bring the pan up to the boil over a medium heat.

Reduce the heat, cover the pan and simmer for 30 minutes or until the fish is tender.

Discard the onions. Take out the eel with a slotted spoon.

Drain it, put into a heated serving dish and keep warm.

In a small bowl, mix the cream and the flour.

Add a little of the hot liquid from the pan.

Blend thoroughly leaving no lumps.

Off the heat, stir this mixture into the sauce in the pan.

Put the pan back on to the heat and stir until the mixture thickens.

Add a pinch of cayenne pepper and a few drops of lemon juice.

Strain the sauce over the fish and serve at once.

PIKE OR ZANDER
WITH PIQUANT SAUCE

Serves 6

Ann Jarman opened the Old Fire Engine House restaurant in Ely in 1968. She serves zander, pike amd eel from the fens as well as game and traditional fods. Zander has a whiter flesh than pike and a milder taste.

2½-3 lbs (1.25-1.50 kg) zander or pike

For the stock:
1 onion
1 carrot
1 bay leaf
A little salt and pepper
A pinch of dried parsley and dill

For the fish:
2 oz (50 g) butter
4 carrots
2 onions
2 glasses of white wine

For the sauce:
2 oz (50 g) butter
1 onion
1 oz (25 g) flour
3 ripe tomatoes
1 dessertspoon of tarragon vinegar
2-3 sliced gerkins
2 tablespoons chopped parsley
A little salt and pepper

Clean the fish, cut off the head, tail, fins and skin it.

Put the fish in a concentrated solution of salt water overnight.

To make the stock:

Put the trimmings of the fish into a saucepan with the onion, carrot, bay leaf, salt, pepper and herbs.

Cover with water and simmer for 30 minutes.

To prepare the fish:

Thinly slice the carrots and onions and put into a shallow dish.

Butter the fish all over and place in the dish.

Pour the wine all over the fish.

Add enough of the stock to come about $^2/_3$ of the way up the fish.

Cover the dish with foil and bake for 30 minutes.

When cooked the flesh of the fish should be a glossy, opaque white.

To make the sauce:

Fry the onion in the butter until soft.

Add the flour and cook for a few minutes.

Remove the cooked fish from the dish and keep it warm on a serving plate under foil.

Strain the stock and gradually add 1 pint (600 ml/ $2^1/_2$ cups) to the roux.

Chop the tomatoes and add to the sauce.

Boil the sauce to concentrate the flavour.

Add the vinegar, gerkins and parsley.

Pour the sauce over the fish and serve immediately.

Oven: 375°/190°C Gas Mark 5

PARTRIDGE POT

Serves 4

Partridges have a delicate flavour. Cooking them in a casserole makes them go further. The season for partridge starts on September 1st and ends on February 1st.

2 partridges
2 oz (50 g) oatmeal
4 oz (100 g) ham or bacon, diced
2 cloves
1 bayleaf
Salt and pepper
4 oz (100 g) mushrooms
1 onion
4 oz (100 g) tomatoes
$^1/_4$ pint (150 ml/ $^2/_3$ cup) red wine or port

Joint the partridges and roll them in the oatmeal.

Boil the neck and any other trimmings in water to make a stock.

Dice the ham or bacon and put in the bottom of a casserole dish. Lay the partridge joints on top of the ham.

Add the cloves, the bayleaf and the salt and pepper.

Slice the onion and the mushrooms and put on top of the meat.

Blanch the tomatoes in boiling water for 1 minute to make them easier to skin.

Skin and chop the tomatoes and add to the casserole.

Pour in the wine or port.

Add enough of the stock to cover the meat.

Cover the casserole with a lid or tin foil and cook for 2$^1/_2$ hours.

Oven: 350°F/180°C Gas Mark 4

ROOK PIE

For the pastry:
6 oz (175 g) plain flour
3 oz (75 g) butter
Salt
A little water

For the filling:
6 rook breasts
8 oz (225 g) rashers streaky or back bacon
2 onions
Salt and pepper
¹/₄ pint (150 ml/ ²/₃ cup) single cream
Milk - enough to cover the filling

To make the filling:

Soak the rook breasts in salted water overnight.

Chop the onions. Layer the rook meat, bacon and onion in a pie dish. Season with salt and pepper.

Add the cream and enough milk to cover the filling.

To make the pastry:

Sieve the flour and salt together.

Rub the butter into the flour until the mixture resembles a breadcrumb mixture.

Add enough cold water to make a soft dough.

Roll out the pastry and place on the pie dish. A pie funnel in the middle will help prevent the crust from falling in.

Bake for 10 minutes then reduce for a further 1 hour.

| Oven: | 425°F/220°C | Gas Mark 7 |
| Reduce to: | 325°F/160°C | Gas Mark 3 |

HEN ON HER NEST

Boiling is an economical method of cooking meat since it produces enough stock to make both a sauce for the meat and also for a soup.

When cooked, the chicken is placed on a bed of rice with hard-boiled eggs hidden underneath to look like a 'hen on her nest.'

1 chicken - 3 lbs (1.5 kg)
1 onion
2 carrots
1 teaspoon ground ginger
1 teaspoon mixed herbs
Salt and pepper
4 oz (100 g) butter
8 oz (225 g) long grain brown rice
4 eggs
2 oz (50 g) flour
$^{1}/_{4}$ pint (150 ml/ $^{2}/_{3}$ cup) double cream

Slice the onion and the carrots.

Put the chicken, onion, carrots, mixed herbs, ginger, salt and pepper into a large saucepan.

Add enough water to cover the chicken completely.

Cover and simmer for 2 hours.

Transfer the chicken to a roasting tin.

Retain the chicken stock.

Spread half of the butter all over the skin.

Put the chicken in a pre-heated oven for 10 minutes to brown the skin.

Remove from the oven and keep warm.

Cook the rice (see below) and hard-boil the eggs.

Make a roux with the flour and remaining butter.

Cook for a few minutes.

Gradually add 1 pint (600 ml/ 2¹/₂ cups) of the chicken stock.

Heat gently until the sauce thickens, stirring all the time.

Stir in the cream.

Arrange the cooked rice on a plate and place the chicken in the centre.

Tuck the hard-boiled eggs underneath.

Pour a little of the sauce over and serve the rest separately.

To cook the rice:

Bring 18 fl oz (550 ml/ 2 cups) water to the boil.

Put in the rice, stir and boil again.

Cover the pan and simmer for 20-25 minutes or until the rice is cooked.

Add salt to taste when the rice is cooked.

Oven: 400°F/200°C   Gas Mark 6

CHICKEN FRICASSEY

Serves 4

4 chicken pieces
Salt and pepper
A bouquet garni
1 oz (25 g) butter
1 oz (25 g) flour
$^{1}/_{2}$ pint (300 ml/ 1$^{1}/_{4}$ cups) cream
2 egg yolks
Half a nutmeg, grated
A wineglassful of white wine
4 oz (100 g) mushrooms

Put the chicken pieces in a large saucepan and just cover with water.

Add salt, pepper and the bouquet garni.

Simmer until the chicken pieces are tender.

Remove them and strain the stock.

In the saucepan make a roux with the flour and the butter.

Cook for a few minutes and then gradually add $^{1}/_{2}$ pint (300 ml/ 1$^{1}/_{4}$ cups) of the stock.

Stir in the cream, grated nutmeg and the wine.

Beat the egg yolks and stir them into the sauce.

Finely chop the mushrooms and add them.

Finally put the chicken pieces back into the saucepan with the sauce.

Heat gently until the sauce has thickened.

Serve immediately.

ROAST GOOSE

Serves 6

Roast goose was traditionally associated with the great Stourbridge Fair held annually in Cambridge during the Middle Ages. The fair specialised in food and at its height it was the most important fair in Europe. Geese have a high proportion of bone to flesh so you need to allow quite a lot of bird per person.

8 lb (3.5 kg) oven-ready goose
Salt
A wineglassful of red wine
$^1/_4$ pint (150 ml/ $^2/_3$ cup) giblet stock

Stand the goose on a rack in a roasting tin.

Pour over the wine and the giblet stock.

Rub salt into the skin.

Put the goose in a pre-heated hot oven for 15 minutes then lower the temperature to a moderate heat and roast for 2 hours (15 minutes per lb/ 450 g.)

During the cooking time baste twice.

20 minutes before the end of the cooking time pour off the juices and fat from the roasting tin and raise the temperature of the oven if necessary to crispen the skin.

The goose is cooked when the juices run clear when pierced with a skewer.

Skim as much fat off the juices as possible and then boil down the meaty juices to make a gravy.

Season the gravy and serve with thin slices of the goose.

Oven: 425°F/220°C   Gas Mark 7
Reduce to: 350°F/180°C   Gas Mark 4

RABBIT STEW

1½-2 lbs (675 g-900 g) jointed rabbit
1 oz (25 g) flour
1 oz (25 g) butter
8 oz (225 g) streaky bacon
2 onions
12 oz (350 g) carrots
2 small turnips
3 sticks of celery
Salt and pepper
1 tablespoon chopped parsley
Water to cover

Roll the rabbit in the flour.

Melt the butter in a large saucepan and fry the rabbit joints until brown all over.

Chop the bacon, onions, celery and turnips.

Slice the carrots.

Add the bacon and vegetables to the saucepan.

Cover with water.

Season with salt, pepper and chopped parsley.

Bring to the boil and simmer for 1 - 1½ hours until the rabbit is tender.

RABBIT PUDDING

For the pastry:
8 oz (225 g) self-raising flour
4 oz (100 g) suet
Approximately ¼ pint (150 ml/ ⅔ cup) water

For the filling:
1 lb (450 g) jointed rabbit
8 oz (225 g) gammon
2 onions
Salt and pepper
Stock (approximately 1 pint (600 ml/ 2½ cups)

To make the pastry:

Sieve the flour and a pinch of salt together. Stir in the suet, gradually adding enough water to make a soft dough.

Roll out two thirds of the dough and use to line a 2 pint (1.15 litre) pudding basin.

To make the filling:

Put the rabbit joints into a saucepan of water and bring to the boil. Lift out the meat, drain and keep on one side.

Dice the gammon and onions.

Layer the rabbit, gammon and onions in the pastry-lined pudding basin and season each layer. Pour in enough stock to cover the filling.

Roll out the remaining pastry. Damp the edges of the pastry and place on top of the pudding basin, pressing the edges together to seal.

Cover the basin with foil pleated in the middle to allow the pudding to rise. Put in a saucepan of water and steam for 4 hours, topping up with water if necessary.

CAMBRIDGE HARE IN ALE

Serves 4-6

1 hare
2 onions
8 oz (225 g) carrots
4 oz (100 g) lard
2 oz (50 g) flour
$\frac{1}{2}$ pint (300 ml/ $1\frac{1}{4}$ cups) brown ale
$\frac{1}{2}$ pint (300 ml/ $1\frac{1}{4}$ cups) stock
Salt and pepper

Joint the hare.

Slice the onions and carrots and fry gently in the lard until soft not allowing them to go brown.

Put them into a casserole dish.

Roll the joints the hare in seasoned flour.

Fry it in the remaining lard until brown all over.

Put it in the casserole dish.

Stir the remaining flour into the remaining lard and cook for a few minutes to make a roux.

Gradually add the stock and ale, stirring until it thickens.

Pour the stock on to the hare and put the lid on.

Cook for $2\frac{1}{2}$ hours.

Oven: 350°F/180°C Gas Mark 4

LAMB CUTLETS

This is an 18th century dish from Cambridge Uiversity.

6 lamb cutlets
1 oz (25 g) lard
3 oz (75 g) streaky bacon
2 onions
2 carrots
3 sticks of celery
A little salt and pepper
³/₄ pint (450 ml/ 2 cups) chicken stock
1¹/₂ lbs (675 g) potatoes
1 oz (25 g) butter
4 tablespoons single cream

Fry the lamb cutlets in the lard until brown all over.

Chop the onions, celery, carrots and bacon and put into the pan with the cutlets.

Fry for a few minutes more but do not let the vegetables brown.

Season with salt and pepper.

Add the stock, cover with a lid and simmer for about 30 minutes.

Transfer to an ovenproof dish.

Boil the potatoes for 15-20 minutes until soft.

Mash the potatoes with the butter and cream.

Spread the creamed potato over the cutlets and bake for abut 15 minutes until well browned.

Serve with tomato sauce.

Oven: 425°/220°C Gas Mark 7

WELSH VENISON

This dish was traditionally served at one of the Cambridge University colleges. Welsh mountain mutton was used and roasted as a haunch of venison would have been - hence the name. The sheep grazed on hills where there was an abundance of wild thyme and the mutton took on the flavour of the herb.

2½ lbs (1.25 kg) boned loin of mutton
A pinch of thyme
Salt and pepper
2 oz (50 g) lard
4 oz (100 g) streaky bacon
4 carrots
2 onions
2 sticks of celery
1 bouquet garni
2 pints (1.15 litres/ 5 cups) brown stock
½ pint (300 ml/ 1¼ cups) port wine
1 oz (25 g) cornflour
Redcurrant jelly

Season the meat with the thyme, salt and pepper, then tie it up securely.

Fry the meat in the lard until brown all over.

Put to one side.

Chop the bacon, carrots, onions, and celery and fry until golden.

Put the bacon and the vegetables into a deep pot with a lid.

Add the bouquet garni and put the meat on top.

Pour the stock over.

Put the lid on and cook in the oven for 2 hours.

Remove the meat and keep warm.

Strain off the vegetables but keep on one side.

Add the wine to the stock and boil vigorously to reduce the liquid.

Blend the cornflour to a thin cream with a little cold water.

Add this to the liquid and heat until it thickens.

Pour the gravy over the meat and serve with the vegetables and redcurrant jelly.

Oven :   300°F/150°C   Gas Mark 2

CAMBRIDGE CABBAGE AND BACON
Serves 4-6

During the Middle Ages many country folk kept their own pig to provide them with pork for sausages and with bacon. Later pigs were not allowed to be kept in homes because of public pressure to improve hygienic conditions.

1 white cabbage
8-12 rashers of a combination of streaky and back bacon
A little butter
Salt and pepper
A pinch of ground mixed spice

Shred the cabbage in boiling water for about 2 minutes.

Drain off the water.

Add a little butter to the cabbage and frazzle until tender.

Chop the bacon and fry in a little butter.

Pile the cabbage in a deep pie dish with the bacon on top.

Season with salt and pepper.

Serve immediately while still hot.

MINCEMEAT PIE

This is not a sweet dish. Mincemeat was originally made using meat and then baked into savoury pie and served as part of the Christmas dinner.

For the pastry:
6 oz (175 g) flour
1¹/₂ oz (40 g) lard
1¹/₂ oz (40 g) butter
A little water
Milk to glaze

For the filling:
1 lb (450 g) shredded suet
8 oz (225 g) meat (traditionally mutton and veal)
1 lb (450 g) currants
Grated rind and juice of 1 lemon
Grated rind and juice of 1 orange
¹/₂ nutmeg, grated
1 tablespoon sugar

To make the pastry:

Rub the lard and butter into the flour until the mixture resembles breadcrumbs.

Add enough water to make a soft dough.

Leave for half an hour before using.

To make the filling:

Mince the meat.

Add the suet, currants, grated rind and juice of the lemon and orange.

Mix all the ingredients until well combined.

Turn into a large pie dish.

Roll out the pastry and cover the ingredients in the pie dish.

Prick the pastry and brush with milk.

Bake for 30 minutes.

Oven: 400°/200°C Gas Mark 6

BACON AND BEANS

Serves 4

Many people in the Middle Ages who kept their own pigs for meat also grew pulses.

8 oz (225 g) dried haricot beans
   or 12 oz (350 g) fresh broad beans
8 oz (225 g) bacon
1 teaspoon chopped parsley
Salt and pepper
2 oz (50 g) melted butter

Soak the haricot beans in water overnight.

Drain them and cover with water in a saucepan.

Boil fast for 10 minutes then simmer, covered, for 45 minutes or until tender. (If you are using broad beans boil in a saucepan until tender).

Meanwhile fry or grill the bacon if using uncooked bacon rashers.

Add the parsley and salt to the beans.

Pour the melted butter over and put the bacon on top.

Serve straight away.

ONION PUDDING OR
ONION CLANGER

Onion Pudding used the same ingredients as Onion Clanger but the two dishes were cooked in slightly different ways. Onion Clanger was made with suet crust pastry which was rolled out, filled with onions and meat and then boiled in a cloth. Onion Pudding, using the same onion and meat mixture, was cooked in a pudding basin lined with suet crust pastry. Onions were sold in great quantities by Flemish immigrants at the Peterborough and Stourbridge (Cambridge) Fairs in the 16th and 17th centuries.

For the suet crust pastry:
8 oz (225 g) self-raising flour
4 oz (100 g) suet
A pinch of salt
Approximately ¼ pint (150 ml/ ⅔ cup) water

For the filling:
6 onions
12 oz (350 g) meat (beef stewing steak/sausages)
1 oz (25 g) flour
¼ pint (150 ml/ ⅔ cup) stock
Salt and pepper

To make the suet crust pastry:

Sieve the flour and salt together.

Stir in the suet.

Gradually add enough water to make a soft dough.

Roll out two-thirds of the dough and, without stretching it, line a 2 pint (1.15 litre) pudding basin.

To make the filling:

Cut the meat into pieces, trimming off any excess fat.

Roll in the flour, seasoned with salt and pepper.

Slice the onions.

Layer the onions and the meat in the basin.

Add the stock.

Roll out the remaining suet crust pastry and lay it over the pudding.

Press the edges together and trim off any excess pastry.

Cover the top with foil pleated in the middle to allow the pudding to rise.

Tie the foil in place with string.

Put into a large saucepan of boiling water and cover with the lid.

Steam for $3^1/_2$ - 4 hours, topping up the water if necessary.

Rope of Onions

MARIGOLD PUDDING

For the suet crust pastry:
8 oz (225 g) self-raising flour
4 oz (100 g) suet
A pinch of salt
Approximately ¼ pint (150 ml/ ⅔ cup) water

For the filling:
1 lb (450 g) stewing steak
8 oz (225 g) pigs kidneys
8 oz (225 g) mushrooms
4 oz (100 g) macaroni
1 pint (600 ml/ 2½ cups) water
Salt and pepper
1 tablespoon Worcester sauce
A dash of Tabasco sauce
1 tablespoon tomato purée

To make the suet crust pastry:

Sieve the flour and salt together.

Stir in the suet.

Gradually add enough water to make a soft dough.

Roll out two-thirds of the dough and, without stretching it, line a 2 pint (1.15 litre) pudding basin.

To make the filling:

Trim any excess fat and gristle from the stewing steak and kidneys and chop into cubes.

Slice the mushrooms.

Fill the basin with layers of stewing steak, kidney, mushrooms and macaroni.

Three-quarters fill the basin with cold water.

Season with salt, pepper, Worcester sauce, Tabasco and tomato purée.

Roll out the remaining pastry. Place on top of the pudding, pressing the edges together and trimming off any excess pastry.

Cover with tin foil, pleated in the middle to allow the pudding to rise.

Tie the foil down with string making a handle at the top.

Put into a large saucepan of boiling water, cover and steam for 4 - 4$\frac{1}{2}$ hours, topping up with water if necessary.

Serve very hot with a mushroom sauce.

CAMBRIDGE SAUSAGE Makes 1¹/₂ lbs (675 g)

There is some controversy over the ingredients used to make the sausage. Some versions include a high percentage of pork and no other meat plus a cereal 'filler'. This particular version uses a variety of meats and no cereal products.

4 oz (100 g) beef
4 oz (100 g) veal
8 oz (225 g) pork
8 oz (225 g) bacon
Salt and pepper
A few sage leaves, chopped

Chop or mince the meat finely.

Season with salt, pepper and sage.

Stuff sausage skins with the meat mixture and twist at regular intervals to make individual sausages.

Fry, grill or bake in the usual way.

You can buy prepared skins from butchers. If you are preparing your own skins you will need pig's intestines. Lay these in a salt and water mixture for 3 days, turn them inside out, scrape and rinse.

The sausage mixture may be cooked without skins as sausage-meat.

Dip the mixture in beaten egg and then in flour, before frying in the usual way.

CROMWELL'S FAVOURITE

Serves 6

Oliver Cromwell was borm in Huntingdon in 1599 and was educated at the Grammar School there. His family owned Hinchingbroke House which is just outside the town.

3 lbs (1.5 kg) boned shoulder of veal
8 oz (225 g) streaky bacon rashers
Salt and pepper
4 oranges
2 oz (50 g) soft brown sugar
2 teaspoons cornflour
A pinch of black pepper
A wineglassful of white wine

Sprinkle the meat with the salt and pepper and put it in a roasting tin.

Lay the bacon rashers over the meat to cover it completely.

Cook in a hot oven for 2 hours and baste frequently.

While the meat is cooking prepare the sauce.

Grate the rind from the oranges and put this and the orange juice into a saucepan with the sugar.

Cook until syrupy, stirring all the time.

Blend the cornflour with a little cold water and stir into the syrup.

Season with the black pepper.

Cook gently until the sauce has thickened.

Add the wine and keep the sauce warm.

When the meat has finished cooking remove the bacon, pour the sauce over the veal and return to the oven for a few minutes.

Serve garnished with orange slices.

Oven: 375°F/190°C Gas Mark 5

HUNTINGDON FIDGET PIE

There is some controversy over the title of this dish. Some sources say that the name comes from the the fact that the contents of the pie visibly 'fidget' under the pie crust while cooking. Another source says that the 'fidget' may have been 'fitchet' which means 'brindled' (brown with streaks of another colour) referring to the colour of the pie rather than its behaviour. It seems that 'fidget' may also have been spelt 'figit' or 'fitchet'.

For the pastry:
6 oz (175 g) plain flour
3 oz (75 g) butter
A pinch of salt

For the filling:
2 onions
1 lb (450 g) cooking apples
1 lb (450 g) back bacon
Salt and pepper
$^1/_4$ pint (150 ml/ $^2/_3$ cup) cider
Egg or milk to glaze

To make the filling:

Chop the onions.

Peel, core and chop the apples.

Cut the bacon into small chunks.

Put the onions, apples and bacon into a pie dish and season with salt and pepper.

Pour the cider over.

To make the pastry:

Sieve the flour and the salt.

Rub the butter into the flour until the mixture resembles breadcrumbs.

Add enough cold water to make a soft dough.

Roll out the pastry and place on top of the dish. A pie funnel will prevent the pastry crust from caving in.

Brush with the egg or milk glaze.

Bake first in a very hot oven for 20 minutes to set the pastry, then turn the heat down to a moderate temperature for a further 30 minutes.

Oven: 425°F/220°C Gas Mark 7
Reduce to: 350°F/180°C Gas Mark 4

DUKE OF CAMBRIDGE TART

Serves 6

This is an old Victorian pudding which is always served cold.

For the pastry:
6 oz (175 g) flour
3 oz (75 g) butter
1 egg

For the filling:
2 oz (50 g) chopped mixed peel
3 oz (75 g) butter
3 oz (75 g) caster sugar
2 egg yolks
A dessertspoon of rum

To make the pastry:

Rub the butter into the flour to make a breadcrumb mixture.

Mix with a beaten egg to bind.

Line an 8 inch (20 cm) flan ring with the pastry and bake blind for 10 minutes in a hot oven.

To make the filling:

Melt the butter in a saucepan.

Stir in the sugar and the egg yolks.

Heat gently but do not let the mixture boil.

Stir in the rum.

Sprinkle the partly baked flan case with the mixed peel and pour the filling on top.

Bake for 40 minutes until golden brown. Serve cold.

| Oven: | 425°F/220°C | Gas Mark 7 |
| Reduce to: | 375°F/190°C | Gas Mark 5 |

PIPPIN TART

Apples were introduced to Cambridgeshire by the Romans and have been grown there ever since. When tomatoes were first introduced into Great Britain they were served as a dessert.

1½ lbs (675 g) Cox's Orange Pippin apples
8 oz (225 g) tomatoes
2 oz (50 g) sugar
8 oz (225 g) puff pastry
¼ pint (150 ml/ ⅔ cup) double cream

Peel, core and slice the apples.

Put into a saucepan with the barest minimum of water just to prevent the pan from burning and cook until stewed.

Blanch the tomatoes in boiling water for 1 minute and remove the skins while still hot.

Purée the tomatoes.

Mix the apples tomatoes and sugar and spoon into a buttered pie dish.

Roll out the puff pastry and cover the pie dish with it.

A pie funnel in the middle will prevent the pastry crust caving in.

Bake for 10-15 minutes in a hot oven, then reduce the heat to moderate and continue cooking for a further 30 minutes.

Serve with the cream.

Oven: 425°F/220°C   Gas Mark 7
Reduce to: 350°F/180°C   Gas Mark 4

DISH OF APPLES

Serves 6

This dish was cooked by Elizabeth Bourchier, wife of Oliver Cromwell. It can be served hot or cold.

For the pastry:
8 oz (225 g) flour
2 oz (50 g) butter
2 oz (50 g) lard
A little cold water to mix

For the filling:
4 oz (100 g) currants
2 lbs (1 kg) Cox's Orange Pippin apples
   (Cooking apples may also be used but a little more sugar
   should be added)
2 oz (50 g) caster sugar
1 teaspoon ground cinnamon
A pinch of caraway seeds
   (optional since they are an acquired taste)
Milk for the glaze

Rub the butter and lard into the flour to make a breadcrumb mixture.

Add a little cold water and mix to a soft dough.

Roll out and line a pie dish with half of the pastry.

Put the currants in a saucepan, cover with a little water and bring to the boil.

While the water is boiling peel and core the apples.

Slice them straight into the water, and boil until they are tender but not reduced to a pulp.

Drain the water from the apples and currants and put the fruit into a pie dish.

Sprinkle with the sugar, cinnamon and the caraway seeds.

Use the rest of the pastry to cover the apple filling, wetting the edges to seal it.

Decorate the edge of the pie as you like, prick the top with a fork and brush it with milk.

Bake for 35 minutes.

Oven: 425°F/220°C Gas Mark 7

POTATO PUDDING

8 oz (225 g) puff pastry
8 oz (225 g) cooked potato
5 oz (150 g) sugar
4 eggs
2 oz (50 g) butter
Grated rind and juice of 1 lemon
A little icing sugar

Roll out the pastry and line a flan dish with it.

Mash the potato to a purée or put through a wire sieve.

Add the butter and stir until it has melted.

Beat the eggs and add to the potato.

Add the grated rind, lemon juice and sugar, and blend well.

Put the potato mixture into the flan dish.

Bake for $^1/_2$ hour until golden brown.

Sprinkle with icing sugar and serve as a dessert.

Oven: 350°F/180°C Gas Mark 4

COLLEGE PUDDING

Serves 6

This is also known as Cambridge Pudding and was served to Cambridge undergraduates as long ago as 1617. It was once cooked in a cloth rather than a pudding basin.

4 oz (100 g) self-raising flour
2 oz (50 g) suet
2 oz (50 g) breadcrumbs
6 oz (175 g) mixed dried fruit
2 oz (50 g) sugar
1 oz (25 g) chopped mixed peel
1 teaspoon mixed spice
1 egg, beaten
$^{1}/_{4}$ pint (150 ml/ $^{2}/_{3}$ cup) milk

Mix all the dry ingredients together with the mixed spice.

Add the beaten egg.

Add the milk gradually to make a mixture that will drop easily from the spoon.

Put the mixture into a greased 2 pint (1.15 litre) pudding basin.

Cover with tin foil pleated in the middle to allow the pudding to rise.

Tie the foil down with string making a handle at the top.

Steam in a large saucepan of boiling water for 2-2$^{1}/_{2}$ hours, topping up the water if necessary.

Allow to cool a little then turn on to a serving plate.

CAMBRIDGE GOLDEN PUDDING Serves 4

4 oz (100 g) chopped suet
2 oz (50 g) breadcrumbs
2 oz (50 g) brown sugar
2 oz (50 g) custard powder
4 oz (100 g) Chivers marmalade
1 teaspoon baking powder
2 eggs
A little milk

Put all the dry ingredients into a bowl.

Make a well in the centre, and add the marmalade.

Beat the eggs and put into the well.

Add enough milk to make a stiff batter.

Grease a 1 lb (450 g) pudding basin.

Turn the mixture into the basin.

Cover with tin foil with a pleat in the middle and tie on with string.

Steam for $2^{1}/_{2}$ -3 hours, topping up with water if necessary.

Turn out and serve hot with marmalade or a marmalade sauce.

GOOSEBERRY PUDDING

Serves 4

Gooseberries are widely grown in Cambridgeshire hence the many local recipes that use gooseberries as the principal ingredient.

For the pastry base:
4 oz (100 g) puff pastry

For the filling:
1 lb (450 g) green gooseberries
2 oz (50 g) brown sugar
¹/₄ pint (150 ml/ ²/₃ cup) water
1 oz (25 g) butter
Grated rind of half a lemon
1 egg yolk, beaten
1 stale sponge cake

For the meringue topping:
2 egg whites
1 tablespoon caster sugar

Line an 8 inch (20 cm) pie dish or flan ring with the puff pastry.

To make the filling:

Top and tail the gooseberries.

Put the gooseberries and the brown sugar into a saucepan with the water, cover and cook gently.

When the gooseberries are soft, liquidize them in a blender or rub them through a wire sieve.

Stir in the butter, lemon rind and egg yolk.

Crumble the sponge cake and add to mixture, blending well. Spoon the gooseberry mixture on to the pastry base.

Bake in a hot oven for 25 minutes.

To make the meringue topping:

Whisk the egg whites until stiff and forming peaks.

Fold in the caster sugar.

Cover the baked gooseberry filling with the meringue and return it to the oven for a further 5 minutes to brown.

Oven: 400°F/200°C Gas Mark 6

GOOSEBERRY CREAM   Serves 6

This is a 17th century recipe.

1 pint (600 ml/ 2¹/₂ cups) double cream
A stick of cinnamon
Grated nutmeg
2 blades of mace
2 oz (50 g) sugar
4 eggs
1 lb (450 g) gooseberries
Icing sugar to dredge

Boil the gooseberries in a little water until tender but do not boil them to a mush.

Put the cream in a saucepan or double boiler with the cinnamon, nutmeg, mace, sugar and eggs.

Very gently bring to boiling point but do not boil or the cream will curdle.

Let it cool and then chill in the fridge.

Put the cream in a shallow circular dish and carefully lay the gooseberries on it in concentric circles.

Sprinkle with icing sugar and serve chilled.

HUNTINGDON PUDDING

4 oz (100 g) self-raising flour
2 oz (50 g) suet
A pinch of salt
1 oz (25 g) caster sugar
¹/₄ pint (150 ml/ ²/₃ cup) milk
8 oz (225 g) gooseberries
2 oz (50 g) brown sugar

Mix the flour, suet and the caster sugar together.

Gradually stir in enough milk to make a soft dropping consistency.

Top and tail the gooseberries.

Grease a 2 pint (1.15 litre) pudding basin.

Starting with a layer of the suet mixture, layer the suet and the gooseberries in the basin, sprinkling each layer of fruit with a little brown sugar.

Finish with a layer of suet.

Cover the basin with tin foil, pleated in the middle.

Tie the foil firmly in place with string, making a handle at the top.

Put the pudding basin in a saucepan of boiling water, cover and simmer for 2 hours.

STRAWBERRY MUSH

Serves 4-6

This delicious dessert is thought to have originated from Clare College, Cambridge.

2 egg whites
4 oz (100 g) caster sugar
1¹/₂-2 lbs (675 g-1 kg) fresh strawberries
1 oz (25 g) icing sugar
3 tablespoons Kirsch
¹/₂ pint (300 ml/ 1¹/₄ cups) double cream

Line a baking tray with greaseproof paper and brush lightly with oil.

Whisk the egg whites until they are stiff and form peaks.

Add half the caster sugar.

Whisk again until stiff and shiny.

Fold in the rest of the caster sugar.

Spoon tablespoonfuls of the mixture on to the baking tray.

Bake in a cool oven for about 2 hours.

The meringues should be white.

When they are cool crush them lightly into pieces.

While the meringues are baking, chop most of the strawberries, leaving a few for decoration.

Sprinkle the strawberries with the sieved icing sugar and the liqueur.

Chill for at least an hour.

Whip the cream stiffly.

Just before serving fold the strawberry mixture and the crushed meringues into the cream and serve decorated with the remaining strawberries.

Oven: 250°F/120°C   Gas Mark ¹/₂

STEWED GOLDEN PIPPINS

1 lb (450 g) Cox's Orange Pippin apples
3 oz (75 g) sugar
1 pint (300 ml/ 1¼ cups) water
The rind and juice of 1 lemon

Peel the apples, quarter them and remove the cores.

Bring the water to the boil.

Add the sugar and the apples.

Boil the fruit vigorously until it is clear.

Add the very finely grated lemon rind and the lemon juice.

TO STEW PEARS   Serves 4

4 pears
½ pint (300 ml/ 1¼ cups) red wine
½ pint (300 ml/ 1¼ cups) water
A few cloves
Sugar to taste

Peel the pears and cut them in half.

Put them in the bottom of a saucepan.

Add the wine, water, cloves and sugar to taste.

Simmer gently until the pears are very soft but have kept their shape.

Remove the cloves.

Serve hot.

GREENGAGE MOULD

Cambridgeshire has its own variety of greengage, called Cambridge Gage.

12 oz (350 g) greengages
3 oz (75 g) brown sugar
3 oz (75 g) cornflour
1¹/₂ pints (900 ml/ 3³/₄ cups) milk

Put the greengages into a saucepan with a little water, just enough to prevent the bottom of the pan from burning.

Boil them until they are tender.

Sieve the fruit, removing the stones at the same time.

Mix the cornflour with a little of the milk to make a smooth paste.

Boil the rest of the milk in a saucepan.

Add the sugar and stir until it is dissolved.

Pour some of the boiling milk on to the cornflour and then return this to the pan.

Stir all the time until the mixture thickens.

Add the greengages and stir over a gentle heat for a few minutes.

Pour into a mould or glass dish and leave to get cold.

Put in the fridge to chill before serving.

GRASSY CORNER PUDDING   Serves 6-8

This dessert was served in some of the University of Cambridge colleges during the 19th century. It makes use of the strawberries that are grown in abundance around Cambridge.

$^1/_4$ pint (150 ml/ $^2/_3$ cup) lemon jelly
8 oz (225 g) pistachio nuts, finely chopped

For the strawberry fruit cream:
1 lb (450 g) strawberries
2 oz (50 g) caster sugar
$^1/_2$ pint (300 ml/ 1$^1/_4$ cups) double cream
$^1/_2$ oz (15 g) gelatine

For the vanilla cream:
$^1/_2$ pint (300 ml/ 1$^1/_4$ cups) milk
3 egg yolks
1 oz (25 g) caster sugar
$^1/_2$ pint (300 ml/ 1$^1/_4$ cups) double cream
$^1/_2$ oz (15 g) gelatine
Vanilla essence

Prepare the lemon jelly.

Leave it until it is just beginning to set.

Line a large mould with half of the setting jelly.

Sprinkle the inside of the mould with chopped pistachio nuts.

Leave in the fridge to set.

To make the strawberry fruit cream:

Put the strawberries in a saucepan with the sugar and the barest minimum of water to prevent the pan from burning and simmer until the strawberries are a pulp.

Sieve the strawberry pulp to make it smooth.

Whip the double cream and stir it into the strawberry pulp.

Dissolve the gelatine in a little water and also stir it into the strawberry pulp.

To make the vanilla cream:

Put the milk, egg yolks and sugar into a double boiler and heat gently until the mixture thickens.

Flavour with a couple of drops of vanilla essence.

Whip the double cream and fold into the custard.

Dissolve the gelatine in a little water and stir into the vanilla cream.

Arrange alternate layers of the strawberry pulp and the vanilla cream in the mould.

Cover with the remaining jelly and leave to set.

Turn out and serve.

RICE PUDDING

2 oz (50 g) ground rice
1 pint (600 ml/ 2¹/₂ cups) milk
3 eggs
Grated rind of 1 lemon
1-2 oz (25 g-50 g) sugar to taste

Put the ground rice and milk in a saucepan and boil until it is smooth.

Let it cool.

Add the eggs, the lemon rind and the sugar to taste.

Put the mixture back on the heat and simmer for ³/₄ - 1 hour.

BURNT CREAM

Serves 6

Burnt Cream is also known by a number of other names such as Cambridge Cream or Trinity Cream, and is similar to the French Creme Brulée. It was introduced to Trinity College in 1879 by a Fellow of the college. It became a great favourite especially associated with May Week, when great ceremony was made of cracking the sugary topping. It needs careful preparation or the cream will curdle.

1 pint (600 ml/ 2¹/₂ cups) double cream
6 egg yolks
1 oz (25 g) caster sugar
2 drops vanilla essence or 1 vanilla pod
Caster sugar for sprinkling on top of the pudding

Put the cream and vanilla in a double boiler.

Bring to boiling point but do not boil.

Allow to cool slightly and remove vanilla pod (if used).

Beat the egg yolks and the sugar together.

Pour the cream on to the eggs and sugar and whisk.

Pour the mixture into a shallow dish and place this in a tin of hot water.

Put in the oven for 30 minutes.

Cool in the fridge until it becomes solid.

Just before serving pre-heat the grill to high.

Sprinkle the pudding with a fine layer of caster sugar.

Place dish in a tray of ice cubes to prevent the pudding from melting.

Grill until the sugar caramelizes to a golden brown.

Watch all the time in case the pudding begins to melt.

Chill again and serve.

Oven: 325°F/160°C   Gas Mark 3

CREAM DARIOLES

Serves 6

Almonds feature in many traditional recipes.

For the dough to line the moulds:
3 oz (75 g) flour
3 oz (75 g) caster sugar
3 oz (75 g) ground almonds
3 egg yolks

For the filling:
$^1/_2$ pint (300 ml/ $1^1/_4$ cups) milk
$^1/_4$ pint (150 ml/ $^2/_3$ cup) double cream
3 eggs
2 oz (50 g) sugar or to taste
Red currant jelly to serve

To make the dough:

Mix the flour, sugar, almonds and egg yolks to make a stiff dough. Roll out and use to line 6 dariole moulds.

Bake these blind for 10 minutes in a hot oven.

To make the filling:

Heat the milk and the cream gently. Beat the eggs and the sugar together.

Pour the milk and the cream on to the eggs and sugar and blend well. Pour into the moulds.

Put the moulds into a tin of hot water and return to the oven at the lower temperature for 20-25 minutes or until set.

Leave them to cool then chill in the fridge. When cold turn out and decorate with redcurrant jelly.

Oven: 400°F/200°C   Gas Mark 6
Reduce to: 350°F/180°C   Gas Mark 4

THE DEAN'S CREAM

This trifle was a favourite pudding of a Dean of Trinity College, Cambridge, in the 19th century. Such was his influence that it appeared on the High Table at all college feasts.

6 oblong trifle sponge cakes
Apricot jam
Raspberry jam
4 oz (100 g) ratafia biscuits or macaroons (crumbled)
$^1/_2$ pint (300 ml/ $^1/_4$ cups) sherry
2 oz (50 g) caster sugar
1 wineglassful of brandy
1 pint (600 ml/ $2^1/_4$ cups) double cream
1 oz (25 g) angelica
4 oz (100 g) glacé cherries
2 oz (50 g) crystallised pineapple

Spread 3 of the sponge cakes with apricot jam and 3 with raspberry jam.

Arrange in a large dish, with jam upwards.

Put the crumbled ratafia biscuits or macaroons on top.

Pour the sherry over and leave for at least half an hour.

Whip together the sugar, brandy and cream until stiff.

Put on top of the cake mixture.

Decorate with cherries, pineapple and angelica.

Chill for at least 1 hour before serving.

CAMBRIDGE SYLLABUB

Serves 4

This is an 18th century recipe that contains no lemon. The cream was poured through a funnel from some height on to the wine to make it frothy. Sweet cider may be used instead of wine.

$^1/_4$ **pint (150 ml/ $^2/_3$ cup) sweet white wine**
2 tablespoons brandy
2 tablespoons caster sugar
$^1/_2$ **pint (300 ml/ 1$^1/_4$ cups) double cream**
Grated nutmeg

Whisk together the wine, brandy and sugar until the sugar dissolves.

Add a pinch of the grated nutmeg.

Whip the cream in gradually until it becomes thick.

Serve in dessert glasses.

Sprinkle with a little more grated nutmeg.

Chill for several hours before serving.

YELLOW FLUMMERY

This needs to be made the night before it is required.

$^1/_2$ oz (15 g) gelatine
1 pint (600 ml/ 2$^1/_2$ cups) water
The grated rind and juice of 1 lemon
$^1/_2$ pint (300 ml/ 1$^1/_4$ cups) white wine
8 egg yolks
2 oz (50 g) sugar

Boil the water with the lemon rind and sprinkle on the gelatine.

Stir until the gelatine has dissolved.

Let it stand until it is cold.

When it is cold add the wine, the egg yolks, the lemon juice and the sugar.

Return to the heat and let it boil for 5 minutes.

Strain it and pour into moulds or glasses which have been dipped in cold water.

Cool then leave to chill in the fridge.

Turn out the flummery if in moulds, and serve.

FLUMMERY

Flummery is a creamy white jelly with a delicate flavour. Serve with fruit such as raspberries, blackberries, strawberries or with whatever is in season.

1 pint (600 ml/ 2¹/₂ cups) cream
The peel from half a lemon pared in strips with
a potato peeler
A stick of cinnamon
2 oz (50 g) caster sugar
2 oz (50 g) ground almonds
2 or 3 drops of almond essence
Flaked almonds for decoration
¹/₂ oz (15 g) gelatine
3 tablespoons cold water

Put the cream, lemon peel, cinnamon stick, sugar, ground almonds and almond essence in a saucepan and heat gently until it just comes to the boil and the sugar has dissolved.

Leave it to cool.

Meanwhile put the gelatine in a small bowl with the water and leave for a couple of minutes.

Put the bowl in a saucepan of simmering water and dissolve the gelatine until it is clear.

Pour the dissolved gelatine into the cream mixture and blend well.

Pour the mixture into a mould and cover with foil.

Put in the fridge overnight to set.

To turn it out dip it quickly into a bowl of hot water.

Serve decorated with flaked almonds.

BUCKDEN PALACE FRUIT CAKE

Makes 2 cakes

The village of Buckden is mentioned in the Domesday Survey of 1086 as Bugedene, a manor belonging to the Bishop of Lincoln. Later a Bishop's residence was built there, which became known as Buckden Palace. The Palace has had several notable visitors through the centuries. Catherine of Aragon stayed there for a year from 1533 to 1534 after the annulment of her marriage to Henry VIII; and Samuel Pepys, who owned properties in the nearby villages of Brampton and Stirloe, was a frequent visitor.

6 oz (175 g) sugar
$\frac{1}{2}$ pint (300 ml/ $1\frac{1}{4}$ cups) water
$1\frac{1}{2}$ oz (40 g) butter
$\frac{1}{2}$ teaspoon cinnamon
$\frac{1}{2}$ teaspoon ground cloves
A pinch of nutmeg
$\frac{1}{2}$ teaspoon salt
1 square bitter chocolate
$\frac{1}{4}$ pint (150 ml/ $\frac{2}{3}$ cup) port wine
1 lb (450 g) raisins
1 lb 12 ozs (800 g) mixed candied fruit
1 oz (25 g) glacé cherries
2 oz (50 g) crystallised pineapple
2 oz (50 g) broken walnuts
2 oz (50 g) broken pecan nuts
2 drops vanilla essence
8 oz (225 g) plain flour
$\frac{1}{2}$ teaspoon bicarbonate of soda
1 teaspoon baking powder

Boil the sugar, water, butter, cinnamon, cloves, nutmeg, salt, chocolate, port, raisins, candied fruit, cherries and the pineapple together slowly for 5 minutes.

Cool and then add the walnuts, pecan nuts, vanilla essence, flour, bicarbonate of soda and the baking powder.

Put the mixture into 2 greased and lined 8 inch (20 cm) cake tins and place the tins in a baking tin of water.

Bake at the higher oven temperature for 1 hour.

Reduce heat to the lower oven temperature and bake for another hour.

Turn off the oven and let the cake cool in the oven.

It is advisable to make the cakes one month before you want to serve them, wrapping them in tin foil or brandy-soaked cloths to age.

Oven: 350°F/180°C   Gas Mark 4
Reduce to: 250°F/120°C   Gas Mark ¹/₂

SEEDE CAKE

This cake was traditionally given to the sowers of wheat on the farmland. It is a Madeira type of cake with the addition of caraway seeds which give it an aniseed flavour.

8 oz (225 g) flour
A pinch of salt
1 teaspoon baking powder
6 oz (175 g) butter
5 oz (150 g) caster sugar
3 eggs, beaten
2-3 tablespoons milk
2 teaspoons caraway seeds

Sift the flour, salt and baking powder together.

Cream the butter and sugar until pale and fluffy.

Gradually beat in the eggs.

Fold in the flour and the caraway seeds.

Add enough milk to make a soft dropping consistency.

Put the mixture into a greased and lined 7 inch (18 cm) cake tin.

Bake for 1 hour.

Leave in the tin for 5 minutes, then turn out on to a wire rack to cool.

Oven: 350°F/180°C   Gas Mark 4

SPICED APPLE CAKE

Serves 6

For the pastry:
6 oz (175 g) flour
4 oz (100 g) butter
1 oz (25 g) caster sugar
$^{1}/_{2}$ teaspoon mixed spice
2 egg yolks

For the filling:
1 lb (450 g) cooking apples
2 oz (50 g) sugar
A cupful of cake crumbs
Grated rind of half a lemon

Rub the butter into the flour. Add the caster sugar and spice.

Bind with the egg yolks to make a soft dough.

Roll out half the pastry and line a flan dish with it.

Sprinkle half of the cake crumbs over the bottom of the flan.

Peel, core and slice the apples.

Put the apples, sugar and lemon rind into a saucepan with the barest minimum of water to stop the pan from burning.

Stew the apples until they form a pulp.

Put the apple mixture into the flan dish.

Cover with the rest of the cake crumbs.

Roll out the rest of the pastry and cover the filling, dampening the edges to join securely.

Bake for 1 hour. Serve cold.

Oven: 350°F/180°C   Gas Mark 4

HISTON TARTLETS

In the early 19th century the Chivers family settled in Histon, a little village near Cambridge, and became fruit farmers. By 1860 the family had 160 acres of land growing fruit. In 1873 in a small barn on the estate the fruit was boiled and made into jam and before long a jam factory was set up. It was at the end of the 19th century that Chivers began preserving fruit in cans.

For the pastry:
4 oz (100 g) plain flour
2 oz (50 g) butter

For the filling:
2 oz (50 g) butter
2 oz (50 g) Chivers apricot jam
1 1/2 oz (40 g) caster sugar
1 egg
2 oz (50 g) cake crumbs
Grated rind and juice of half a lemon
   or 1 oz (25 g) lemon curd

For the topping:
4 oz (100 g) icing sugar
The juice of half a lemon
Chopped pistachio nuts

To make the pastry:

Sieve the flour and rub in the butter until the mixture resembles breadcrumbs.

Add enough water to make a soft dough.

Roll out the pastry thinly and line 12 patty tins.

To make the filling:

Put a little apricot jam in each pastry lined patty tin.

Cream together the butter, caster sugar, the cake crumbs and the egg.

Gradually add the grated lemon rind and the lemon juice or the lemon curd.

Almost fill each patty tin with mixture and bake in a moderate oven for 30 - 35 minutes or until the tartlets are a pale golden brown.

When the tartlets are cold make the icing.

To make the icing:

Sieve the icing sugar.

Gradually add the lemon juice to give a thick flowing consistency.

Spoon the icing on top of the tartlets and sprinkle them with the chopped pistachio nuts.

Oven: 350°F/180°C   Gas Mark 4

RICE CAKE

6 oz (175 g) butter
6 oz (175 g) caster sugar
4 oz (100 g) ground rice
6 oz (175 g) flour
1 teaspoon baking powder
4 eggs

Mix all the ingredients together thoroughly.

Bake in a greased 7 inch (18 cm) cake tin for about $1^1/_4$ hours.

Oven: 350°F/180°C   Gas Mark 4

LARDY CAKE

Also known as Sharley Cake. It was traditionally baked in a circular cake tin and served for tea at weekends.

1 lb (450 g) plain flour
2 teaspoons salt
$^{1}/_{2}$ oz (15 g) fresh yeast/ 2 teaspoons dried yeast
1 teaspoon sugar
$^{1}/_{2}$ pint (300 ml/ 1$^{1}/_{4}$ cups) water (hand-hot)
10 oz (275 g) lard
4 oz (100 g) caster sugar
1 oz (25 g) currants
1 oz (25 g) sultanas
$^{1}/_{4}$ teaspoon grated nutmeg
$^{1}/_{4}$ teaspoon cinnamon
$^{1}/_{4}$ teaspoon mixed spice
Milk for the glaze

Dissolve the teaspoon of sugar in the warm water, add the yeast and whisk.

Leave in a warm place for about 10 minutes.

Add the sifted flour and salt to the yeast mixture.

Knead for about 10 minutes or until smooth.

Put in an oiled polythene bag or in a bowl covered with a damp cloth and leave in a warm place until doubled in size.

Roll the dough into a rectangular shape about $^{1}/_{2}$ inch (1 cm) thick.

Dot with $^{1}/_{3}$ of the lard all over the dough and sprinkle with $^{1}/_{3}$ of the caster sugar.

Fold the dough into 3 or roll up loosely.

Turn the dough round and roll out again from the open end.

Dot with $^{1}/_{3}$ lard and sprinkle with $^{1}/_{3}$ caster sugar.

Fold or roll the dough then roll out again.

Cover with remaining lard, sugar, currants, sultanas and mixed spice.

Roll the dough out to fit a greased 9 inch (23 cm) cake tin.

Mark the top of the dough into a wide criss-cross pattern ready for breaking into pieces when cooked.

Put the cake back into the oiled polythene bag or re-cover with damp cloth.

Leave to rise again until doubled in size.

Brush with milk.

Bake in a hot oven for 20-25 minutes.

Leave in the tin for a few minutes.

Cool on a wire rack.

Lardy cake is traditionally broken, not cut, along the marked criss-cross lines and is delicious served with butter and jam.

Oven: 425°F/220°C   Gas Mark 7

FOURSES CAKE

Makes two 1 lb cakes

When the farmworkers were at work in the fields they were served with cakes and ale in the afternoon at about four o'clock - hence the name of this cake, which is more like a sweet bread than a cake as we know it today.

1 lb (450 g) plain flour
2 teaspoons salt
1 teaspoon mixed spice
¹/₂ teaspoon sugar
4 oz (100 g) lard
¹/₂ oz (15 g) fresh yeast or 2 teaspoons dried yeast
¹/₂ pint (300 ml/ 1¹/₄ cups) warm water
8 oz (225 g) currants

Dissolve the sugar in the water which should be hand-hot.

Sprinkle on the yeast and leave for about 10 minutes until frothy.

Sift the flour and add the salt and mixed spice.

Rub in the lard.

Pour the yeast mixture on to the flour and lard and mix well to make an elastic dough.

Knead well for about 10 minutes and put into an oiled polythene bag or into a bowl covered with a damp cloth and leave in a warm place until it has doubled in size.

Knock the dough back and knead in the currants.

Shape into 2 loaves and put into two greased 1 lb (450 g) loaf tins.

Return to the oiled polythene bag or covered bowl and leave to rise again.

Bake in a hot oven for 45 minutes.

Oven: 400°F/200°C   Gas Mark 6

CHRISTMAS CAKE

12 oz (350 g) flour
1 teaspoon mixed spice
1 nutmeg, grated
A pinch of salt
8 oz (225 g) dark brown sugar
2 lbs (1 kg) mixed dried fruit
2 oz (50 g) candied peel, chopped
2 oz (50 g) ground almonds
8 oz (225 g) butter
5 eggs, beaten
3 tablespoons brandy

Sieve the flour, mixed spice, nutmeg and salt together.

Mix the sugar, dried fruit, candied peel and the almond into the flour mixture.

Beat the butter until pale in colour and gradually add the beaten eggs.

Stir in the brandy.

Add the dried fruit and flour mixture to the eggs and butter.

Mix together thoroughly.

Put into a large greased and lined cake tin or into 2 tins.

Bake for 3-3$^{1}/_{2}$ hours.

Oven: 300°F/150°C   Gas Mark 2

CAMBRIDGE TEA LOAF

6 oz (175 g) butter
8 oz (225 g) self-raising flour
2 oz (50 g) caster sugar
8 oz (225 g) mixed fruit
2 oz (50 g) chopped mixed peel
2 oz (50 g) chopped walnuts
$\frac{1}{4}$ teaspoon cinnamon
Salt
Approximately $\frac{1}{4}$ pint (150 ml/ $\frac{2}{3}$ cup) milk

Rub the butter into the flour.

Add the rest of the ingredients.

Mix well together.

Grease a 2 lb (1 kg) loaf tin.

Spoon the mixture into the tin.

Bake in a moderate oven for 1 hour 20 minutes.

Oven: 350°F/180°C   Gas Mark 4

GOOSEBERRY CHUTNEY

Makes about 4 lbs (1.75 kg)

3 lbs (1.5 kg) gooseberries
1 lb 12 oz (800 g) demerara sugar
4 onions
8 oz (225 g) raisins
2 tablespoons salt
1 teaspoon crushed mustard seed
$^1/_2$ teaspoon cayenne pepper
$^1/_4$ teaspoon turmeric
$1^1/_2$ pints (900 ml/ $3^3/_4$ cups) vinegar

Top and tail the gooseberries.

Chop the onions.

Put all the ingredients into a large saucepan.

Bring to the boil and then simmer for $1^1/_2$ -2 hours or until the mixture thickens.

Pour it into sterilised glass jars.

Cover when the chutney is cool.

Seal tightly.

STRAWBERRY JAM

Makes about 4-5 lbs (1.75-2.25 kg)

3 lbs (1.5 kg) fresh, firm strawberries
3 lbs (1.5 kg) granulated sugar
The juice of 1 lemon

Hull the strawberries.

Put the strawberries and lemon juice into a large saucepan or preserving pan and heat gently for 5 minutes.

Meanwhile warm the sugar in a dish in a low oven for 5 minutes.

Add the warmed sugar to the strawberries and stir continuously until it dissolves.

Bring the mixture to the boil and boil until setting point is reached (when a teaspoon of jam dropped on to a cold plate will set in a minute with a wrinkled skin).

Do not overboil or the jam will lose its clear red colour.

Skim and cool until a skin starts to form on the jam.

Pour into hot sterilised jars and seal.

Oven: 300°F/ 150°C   Gas Mark 2

REDCURRANT JELLY

Makes about 3lbs (1:15 kg)

3 lbs (1.5 kg) redcurrants
1 pint (600 ml/ 2¹/₂ cups) water
Sugar

Simmer the redcurrants and the water in a large saucepan until tender (this will take about ¹/₂ hour).

Put into three thicknesses of muslin and leave to strain without squeezing.

Measure the liquid and pour it back into the pan.

Add 1 lb (450 g) sugar for each 1 pint (600 ml/ 2¹/₂ cups) of liquid.

Heat gently until the sugar has dissolved.

Boil for about 15 minutes until the setting point has been reached. (To test for setting point put a teaspoon of the jelly on to a cold saucer. Leave to cool. If setting point has been reached the skin of the jam should wrinkle when you push it gently with your finger.)

Pour into warmed sterilised jars.

Put wax or greaseproof discs on the jelly and then cover the jars.

Serve with Cream Darioles (see recipe). It is also delicious with lamb, game and chicken.

SWEET CHESTNUT JAM

Makes 2-3 lbs (1 - 1.5 kg)

2 lbs (900 g) whole sweet chestnuts
1½ lb (675 g) preserving sugar
½ pint (300 ml/ 1¼ cups) water
2 tablespoons vanilla essence

To peel the chestnuts make a slit with a knife in the skin of each one and put them into a wire basket, then put this into a saucepan of boiling water.

After a few minutes lift the basket out and peel off the outer and inner skins of the chestnuts while they are still warm.

Boil the peeled chestnuts in water for about 20 minutes until soft.

Blend them to a purée in a liquidizer or rub them through a wire sieve.

Dissolve the sugar in the water over a gentle heat and add the vanilla essence.

Add the puréed chestnuts and cook until the mixture is thick.

Put into scrupulously clean and sterilized jars, cover with waxed paper discs and seal when the jam is cool.

The jam should keep for about 2 weeks.

It is best kept in the fridge.

Sweet chestnut jam is so delicious that eating it within 2 weeks will not be a problem.

ORANGE FLOWER CUSTARD

Makes about 1 pint (600 ml/ 2¹/₂ cups)

Orange flower water and rose water were commonly used as subtle flavouring in the 18th and 19th centuries.

2 egg yolks
1 pint (600 ml/ 2¹/₂ cups) milk or cream
2 tablespoons orange flower water
(available from chemists)
A little grated nutmeg
A little sugar to taste

Beat the egg yolks.

Gradually add them to the milk or cream.

Put on a low heat or in a double boiler and stir until it thickens.

Add the orange flower water, a pinch of grated nutmeg and sugar to taste.

A tablespoon of curacao may be used instead of the orange flower water.

CAMBRIDGE SAUCE

4 hard-boiled egg yolks
3 tablespoons olive oil
2 tablespoons tarragon vinegar
The juice of 1 lemon
Salt
A pinch of cayenne pepper
1 teaspoon of English mustard, dry
4 chopped anchovy fillets
1 teaspoon chopped capers
1 teaspoon chopped tarragon
1 teaspoon chopped chervil

Pound the hard-boiled egg yolks.

Whisk the olive oil, vinegar and lemon juice until thick.

Add salt, cayenne pepper and mustard to taste.

Add the egg yolks, the chopped anchovy fillets, chopped capers tarragon and chervil.

Leave for at least $1/2$ hour before serving.

BRANDY BUTTER OR
SENIOR WRANGLER SAUCE

From the mid-18th century any Cambridge Undergraduate who was awarded a first class pass in their maths tripos was also given the title of 'wrangler'. The student who obtained the highest mark of all the wranglers was named the 'senior wrangler'. A Master of Trinity College in the mid-19th century who was also a senior wrangler gave this name to Brandy Butter.

6 oz (175 g) unsalted butter
6 oz (175 g) caster sugar
4-5 tablespoons brandy to taste

Cream the butter.

Gradually beat in the sugar.

Beat or whisk until the mixture is white.

Beat in the brandy 1 tablespoon at a time.

Chill before serving.

Good served with mince pies and Christmas Pudding.

APPLE AND PRUNE STUFFING

This is an excellent stuffing for roast goose.

4 oz (100 g) fresh brown breadcrumbs
8 prunes, soaked
2 apples
1 oz (25 g) hazelnuts
Salt and pepper
The juice of 1 lemon
1 oz (25 g) butter, melted
1 egg

Stone and chop the prunes.

Peel, core and chop the apples.

Chop the hazelnuts.

Put the breadcrumbs, prunes, apples and hazelnuts into a bowl.

Season with salt and pepper.

Add the lemon juice, and the melted butter.

Beat the egg and stir into the mixture to bind it together.

Put the stuffing into the cavity of the prepared goose.

CHESTNUT STUFFING

Chestnut stuffing is traditionally used to stuff turkey.

1 lb (450 g) chestnuts
½ pint (300 ml/ 1¼ cups) milk
2 oz (50 g) butter
4 oz (100 g) breadcrumbs
4 oz (100 g) bacon rashers (chopped)
2 apples (chopped)
Finely chopped parsley
Salt and pepper
1 egg

Make a slit in each nut and put in boiling water for a few minutes.

Remove from the water and while still hot peel off both the skins (inner and outer).

Put the peeled chestnuts in a saucepan with the milk and cook for 15-20 minutes until tender.

Mash the chestnuts, with the butter, breadcrumbs, chopped bacon, chopped apples, parsley, salt and pepper.

Bind together with a beaten egg.

NETTLE BEER

Makes about 8 pints (4.5 litres)

This was frequently made by families during the Spring for use during the Summer. It was claimed that the beer was cooling and health giving.

2 lbs (1 kg) young nettles
1 gallon (4.5 litres/ 20 cups) water
1 lb (450 g) demerara sugar
1 oz (25 g) cream of tartar
The juice and rind of 2 lemons
1 oz (25 g) fresh yeast

Boil the nettles in the water for 15-20 minutes.

Strain off the nettles.

Add the sugar, cream of tartar and the juice and rind of the lemons to the nettle liquid.

Stir until the sugar has dissolved.

Leave to cool until the temperature is hand-hot.

Add the yeast.

Cover and keep in a warm place for three days.

Strain the beer into bottles and cork firmly.

Leave the beer for a week before drinking.

TRINITY HALL CIDER CUP

Makes about 6 pints (3.5 litres/ 15 cups)

Trinity Hall is one of the Cambridge University colleges and is situated next to Trinity College.

2 bottles cider
1 bottle Madeira
¼ pint (150 ml/ ⅔ cup) brandy
¼ pint (150 ml/ ⅔ cup) sherry
¼ pint (150 ml/ ⅔ cup) rum
1 tablespoon sugar in 4 tablespoons water
The juice of ½ lemon
A thin slice of dried toast sprinkled with grated nutmeg.

Make a syrup by dissolving the sugar in the water.

Mix all the ingredients together.

Decorate with the toast.

CAMBRIDGE ALE CUP

Makes about 6 pints (3.5 litres/ 15 cups)

The Cambridge University colleges at one time brewed their own ale in their college brewhouses.

3 pints (1.75 litres/ 6 cups) water
1 oz (25 g) cloves
1 oz (25 g) cinnamon
1 oz (25 g) mace
4 tablespoons sugar
The juice of 1 lemon
3 pints (1.75 litres/ 6 cups) brown ale
½ pint (300 ml/ 1¼ cups) sherry

Thin slices of toast sprinkled with grated nutmeg

Bring the water, cloves, cinnamon and mace to the boil in a large saucepan.

Simmer for 1 hour.

Strain the liquid and add the sugar, lemon juice, brown ale and sherry.

Heat just before serving and float the toast sprinkled with grated nutmeg on top.

RUM BOOZE

This punch is associated with Christ's College, Cambridge.

4 egg yolks, beaten
2 tablespoons caster sugar
$^1/_2$ bottle of sherry
The grated rind of $^1/_2$ lemon
$^1/_2$ nutmeg, grated
1 stick of cinnamon
A glass of rum

Mix the beaten egg yolks and the sugar in a large saucepan.

Add the sherry, lemon rind, grated nutmeg and cinnamon stick.

Slowly bring to the boil and then remove from heat.

Pour into a jug or punch bowl.

Add the glass of rum, gradually, whisking the punch to form a froth.

Serve immediately.

CAMBRIDGE MILK PUNCH
Makes about 6 pints (3.5 litres/ 15 cups)

Hot punches such as this milk punch were served in the University of Cambridge at the Christmas festivities.

4 pints (2.25 litres/ 10 cups) milk
The peel of 1 lemon
4 oz (100 g) sugar
2 eggs
1 pint (600 ml/ 2$^{1}/_{2}$ cups) rum
$^{1}/_{2}$ pint (300 ml/ 1$^{1}/_{4}$ cups) brandy

Put 3$^{1}/_{2}$ pints (2 litres/ 9 cups) of the milk, lemon peel and the sugar into a large pan.

Bring it slowly to the boil.

Remove from the heat and take out the lemon peel.

Whisk the eggs with the remaining milk.

Gradually stir into the hot milk.

Gradually add the rum and the brandy.

Return the punch to the heat and whisk until it is frothy.

Serve immediately.

JESUS COLLEGE MILK PUNCH

Jesus College, Cambridge had its own version of the popular hot milk punch.

2 pints (1.15 litres/ 5 cups) milk
3 oz (75 g) sugar
The peel of 1 lemon
1 nutmeg, grated
6 eggs
½ pint (300 ml/ 1¼ cups) rum

Slowly bring milk, sugar, lemon peel and grated nutmeg to the boil.

Strain off the lemon peel.

In a large bowl beat the eggs.

Pour the milk mixture on to the eggs stirring all the time.

Add the rum.

Pour into a warmed punch-bowl from a height to make it frothy.

Serve immediately.

BISHOP

Hot spiced port was popular in the University of Cambridge and was known as 'Bishop'. It was referred to as: "Port wine made copiously potable by being mulled and burnt with the addenda of roasted lemons all bristling like angry hedgehogs (studded with cloves) ..."

1 bottle port wine
1 lemon
6 cloves
A pinch of mixed spice
Grated nutmeg
$^1/_2$ pint (300 ml/ $1^1/_4$ cups) water

Make several pricks in the lemon and stick in the cloves.

Roast the lemon in a low oven or over a slow fire for 30 minutes.

Put the water and the mixed spice in a saucepan.

Boil until the quantity of liquid is reduced by half.

Put the port wine in another saucepan.

Heat rapidly to burn off some of the spirit.

Put the roasted lemon and the hot spiced liquid into the port wine.

Heat gently for about 10 minutes.

Sprinkle with grated nutmeg and serve warm to hot.

Oven: 300°F/150°C   Gas Mark 3

ELDERBERRY WINE

3 lbs (1.5 kg) elderberries
1 lb (450 g) raisins
3 lbs (1.5 kg) sugar
½ oz (15 g) citric acid
Wine yeast
Yeast nutrient
1 gallon (4.5 litres) water

Remove all the stalks from the elderberries.

Boil the water.

Crush the elderberries.

Mince the raisins.

Put the elderberries and the raisins together and pour the boiling water over them.

Allow the liquid to cool to hand-hot temperature.

Add the yeast, the yeast nutrient and the citric acid.

Cover and leave in a warm place for three days, stirring daily.

Put the sugar into a bowl.

Strain the fermenting wine on to the sugar.

Pour this into a stone jar or a dark glass bottle.

Do not fill completely.

When the fermenting has subsided, top up the bottles or jars with cold boiled water and fit a fermentation lock.

Leave until the fermentation has finished and then siphon off into clean, dark bottles and keep them in a dark cupboard to preserve the dark red colour of the wine.

PARSNIP WINE

4 lbs (1.75 kg) parsnips
1 gallon (4.5 litres) water
3 lbs (1.5 kg) sugar
1 tablespoon fresh yeast

Cut the parsnips into slices.

Boil them in the water until they are very soft.

Strain and keep the liquid.

Add the sugar to the strained liquid.

Boil the liquid for ³/₄ hour.

Leave to cool until the liquid is hand-hot.

Add the yeast and leave it to ferment for 36 hours.

Fill a cask with the liquid and leave for 6 months without moving it.

This wine will improve with time.

THE COUNTRY RECIPE SERIES

Available now @ £1.95 each

Cambridgeshire
Devon
Dorset
Hampshire
Kent
Somerset
Sussex
Yorkshire

Coming May 1988

Cornwall
Cumberland & Westmorland
Lancashire
Norfolk

All these books are available at your local bookshop or newsagent, or can be ordered direct from the publisher. Just tick the titles you require and fill in the form below. Prices and availability subject to change without notice.

Ravette Limited, 3 Glenside Estate, Star Road, Partridge Green, Horsham, West Sussex RH13 8RA.

Please send a cheque or postal order, and allow the following for postage and packing. UK 25p for one book and 10p for each additional book ordered.

Name ....

Address...

....

....

Acknowledgements:

Grateful thanks are extended to the many people of Cambridgeshire who have contributed towards this collection of recipes including:

Chivers Hartley Division of Premier Brands UK Limited for Cambridge Golden Pudding and Histon Tartlets.

The Reverend J. Fischer, formerly of Buckden Palace, for Buckden Palace Fruit Cake.